SECURING THE HOMELAND STRENGTHENING THE NATION

PRESIDENT GEORGE W. BUSH

Table of Contents

September 11, 2001, and its Aftermath

Our Nation learned a painful lesson on September 11. American soil is not immune to evil or cold-blooded enemies capable of unprecedented acts of mass murder and terror. The worst of these enemies – and target number one in our war on terrorism – is the terrorist network Al Qaeda. Yet the threat to America is not limited to Al Qaeda – or to suicide hijackings of commercial aircraft. As we learned on October 4, 2001, a Florida man named Robert Stevens became the first known victim of an unprecedented act of biological terrorism.

A new wave of terrorism, involving new weapons, looms in America's future. It is a challenge unlike any ever faced by our Nation. But we are not daunted. We possess the resources and the determination to defeat our enemies and work to secure our homeland against the threats they pose.

The Terrorist Threat: A Permanent Condition

Today's terrorists can strike at any place, at any time, and with a wide variety of weapons. The most urgent terrorist threat to America is the Al Qaeda network. We will prosecute our war with these terrorists until they are routed from the Earth. But we will not let our guard down after we defeat Al Qaeda. The terrorist threat to America takes many forms, has many places to hide, and is often invisible. We can never be sure that we have defeated all of our terrorist enemies, and therefore we can never again allow ourselves to become overconfident about the security of our homeland.

There are two inescapable truths about terrorism in the 21st century.

- First, the characteristics of American society that we cherish – our freedom, our openness, our great cities and towering skyscrapers, our modern transportation systems – make us vulnerable to terrorism of catastrophic proportions. America's vulnerability to terrorism will persist long after we bring justice to those responsible for the events of September 11.

- Second, the technological ability to launch destructive attacks against civilian populations and critical infrastructure spreads to more and more organizations and individuals with each passing year. This trend is an unavoidable byproduct of the technological, educational, economic, and social progress that creates jobs, wealth, and a good quality of life.

The combination of these two facts means the threat of terrorism is an inescapable reality of life in the 21st century. It is a permanent condition to which America and the entire world must adjust.

The need for homeland security, therefore, is not tied to any specific terrorist threat. Instead, the need for homeland security is tied to the underlying vulnerability of American society and the fact that we can never be sure when or where the next terrorist conspiracy against us will emerge. The events of September 11 were a harsh wake-up call to all citizens, revealing to us the danger we face. Not since World War II have our American values and our way of life been so threatened. The country is now at war, and securing the homeland is a national priority.

A New National Calling: Homeland Security

The higher priority we all now attach to homeland security has already begun to ripple through the land. The Government of the United States has no more important mission than fighting terrorism overseas and securing the homeland from future terrorist attacks. This effort will involve major new programs and significant reforms by the Federal government. But it will also involve new or expanded efforts by State and local governments, private industry, non-governmental organizations, and citizens. By working together we will make our homeland more secure.

Furthermore, as we pursue the goals of homeland security we will build an America better and stronger than it was before. Out of the crisis triggered by September 11 has emerged a renewed commitment by all Americans to their country. We will transform the adversity of September 11 into greater opportunities for the future. We will channel America's renewed civic spirit into concrete improvements in our society. We will find new and important ways to encourage citizens to be more alert and active in their communities. We will renovate our inadequate public safety systems – most importantly public health – and will enhance America's emergency management system. We will consider new organizational models for governing that are appropriate for the new century. We will promote the principles and practice of mutual aid across America. And we will provide leadership and technical assistance to our international partners who seek greater security in their own homelands.

The American people should have no doubt that we will succeed in weaving an effective and permanent level of security into the fabric of a better, safer, stronger America.

America's Response to Date

An unprecedented national response to the present terrorist threat began literally minutes after the first plane struck the World Trade Center. Virtually every American has been involved in one way or another. Some rushed into burning buildings, putting themselves in harm's way to save the lives of others. Others demonstrated their solidarity by wearing an American flag in their lapel. Some flew combat air patrols over our cities; some fought overseas. Others ministered to the sick and comforted the grieving.

Virtually every sector of American society exhibited courage and responsibility by addressing the security needs of the people. At the Federal level, Congress appropriated a $40 billion Emergency Response Fund to wage war against Al Qaeda, aid the reconstruction efforts in New York and Virginia, compensate victims, and strengthen our defenses at home. A total of $10.6 billion was dedicated to homeland security, which has allowed the Federal government to:

- increase the number of sky marshals on our airlines;

- acquire enough medicine to treat up to 10 million more people for anthrax or other bacterial infection;

- distribute $1.1 billion to States to strengthen their capacity to respond to bioterrorism and other public health emergencies resulting from terrorism;

- deploy hundreds of Coast Guard cutters, aircraft, and small boats to patrol the approaches to our ports and protect them from internal or external threats;

- acquire equipment for certain major mail sorting facilities to find and destroy anthrax bacteria and other biological agents of terror; and

- station 8,000 National Guard at baggage screening checkpoints at 420 major airports.

The Emergency Response Fund also supported the largest criminal investigation in United States history. This investigation has been greatly assisted by another act of Congress – the passage of the "USA Patriot Act," signed into law by the President on October 26, 2001. In essence, the legislation dealt with four broad areas:

1. Federal criminal laws were updated to reflect the rapid and dramatic changes that have taken place in recent years in communications technology. For example, it improved law enforcement's ability to obtain stored voice mail and records from communications and computer-service providers, and amended the pen register/trap and trace statute to apply to Internet communications.

2. Important measures were adopted to combat money laundering. For instance, it required the Department of the Treasury to promulgate rules requiring financial institutions to verify the identities of persons opening accounts, granted immunity to financial institutions that voluntarily disclosed suspicious transactions, and increased the penalties for money-

laundering. These authorities permitted the Federal government to investigate the sources of terrorist funding – and then freeze the financial assets of more than 150 individuals and organizations connected to international terrorism.

3. The ability of the Immigration and Naturalization Service was enhanced to detain or remove suspected terrorists at the Nation's borders. It broadened the terrorism-related definitions in the Immigration and Nationality Act; expanded the grounds of inadmissibility to include aliens who publicly endorse terrorist activity; required the Attorney General to detain aliens whom he certifies as threats to national security; gave the Secretary of State discretion to provide visa records to foreign governments for the purpose of combating international terrorism or crime; and required the Federal Bureau of Investigation to share criminal record information with the INS and the State Department for the purpose of adjudicating visa applications.

4. The law authorized grants that will enhance State and local governments' ability to respond to and prevent terrorism, and expanded information-sharing among law enforcement authorities at different levels of government.

Additionally, since September 11, the Administration has gone to great lengths to identify the most vulnerable potential targets and critical infrastructure in America, and then to put in place appropriate additions safeguards and security procedures. These potential targets include airports, sea and water ports, nuclear facilities, dams, water and sewer plants, electric power plants, gas pipelines, dams and bridges and biological and chemical facilities. The Administration has also paid extra attention to high-profile events such as the Olympics and the Super Bowl, and has responded vigorously to intelligence reports of possible terrorist threats.

Yet it has not been just the Federal government responding to the terrorist threat. Precise figures are not available, but the National Governors Association has estimated that States have spent at least $650 million to help protect their citizens. These expenditures have gone to protect critical infrastructure facilities as described above. Additionally, the border States have shared with the Federal government the responsibility for bolstering America's land borders and increasing security at vulnerable points of entry.

Local governments have played a critical role in securing their respective communities as well. Local police, fire, and emergency personnel have worked tirelessly since September 11 to ensure the safety and security of their citizens. They are carrying a burden unforeseen prior to the 2001 attacks on America. Local governments have recognized the importance of these men and women and remain committed to their most critical mission of public safety. According to the U.S. Conference of Mayors, initial estimates show that local communities have spent more than $525 million for added security. Moreover, they anticipate that these cities will spend about $2.1 billion in 2002 on heightened security. It is evident that new equipment purchases, overtime expenses, and responding to threats in America's urban, suburban and rural communities (both actual emergencies and hoaxes), have required significant – but much needed – new outlays by local governments.

National Strategy for Homeland Security

> "The mission of the Office [of Homeland Security] shall be to develop and coordinate the implementation of a comprehensive national strategy to secure the United States from terrorist threats or attacks."
>
> President George W. Bush, Executive Order 13228, Section 2, October 8, 2001

The United States has never had a national blueprint for securing itself from the threat of terrorism. This year, with the publication of the National Strategy for Homeland Security, it will.

The President has directed Governor Tom Ridge, Director of the Office of Homeland Security, to develop the National Strategy for Homeland Security. The process by which this document is generated, however, will involve consultation with literally hundreds of people, including officials from all relevant Federal agencies, the Congress, State and local governments, as well as the best experts in private industry and at institutions of higher learning.

Homeland Security is a challenge of monumental scale and complexity. It will not be cheap, easy, or quick. Achieving our homeland security objectives will require hard work and a sustained investment of money and time. Our job has already begun and will continue indefinitely. A carefully conceived plan is required to ensure that these efforts yield maximum-security benefits at the least possible financial and social cost.

√ The strategy will be long-term. It will not seek to achieve all goals at once but will introduce needed reforms and innovations in stages, according to their importance. It will seek to ensure that improvements put in place one year become permanent.

√ The strategy will be a truly national plan, not just a Federal government strategy. The nature of American society and the structure of American governance make it impossible to achieve the goal of a secure homeland through Federal activity and expense alone. The National Strategy for Homeland Security, therefore, will be based on the principle of partnership with State and local governments, the private sector, and citizens.

√ The strategy will be comprehensive. It will encompass the full range of homeland security activities and will set priorities among them.

√ The strategy will utilize all appropriate policy options for achieving a more secure homeland. The strategy will direct the expenditure of the taxpayers' money only after proper analysis has been done to ensure that the money will be well spent. So in addition to new or expanded Federal programs, the strategy will also call for government reorganization, legal reform, regulation and tax incentives, cost-sharing arrangements with State and local governments, cooperative arrangements with the private sector, and the organized involvement of citizens.

√ The strategy will seek opportunity out of adversity. We will build, for example, an emergency management system that is better able to manage not just terrorism but all hazards; a medical system that is not just better able to cope with bioterrorism but with all diseases and all manner of mass-casualty incidents; and a border management system that is not just better able to stop terrorist penetration but more efficient for legitimate traffic.

√ The strategy will set clear objectives for homeland security toward which the Nation can strive, and will include benchmarks and other performance measures by which we can evaluate our progress and allocate resources.

√ The strategy will be supported by a multi-year, cross-cutting Federal budget plan. The Budget for 2003 is a down payment on a larger set of homeland security initiatives that will be described in the national strategy and reflected in the 2004 and later budgets.

The strategy will take full account of the existing government institutions and systems for providing homeland security, such as law enforcement, public safety, public health, and emergency management. The strategy will reflect the basic management principle that individual agencies' responsibilities and authorities for homeland security should be clearly and logically aligned with their core competencies. It will build upon systems that currently work well and are sensibly organized, but will also lay out plans to improve those that either do not work well today or are poorly or redundantly organized.

Homeland Security and the 2003 Budget

The President's Budget for 2003 – the Federal government's first post-September 11 budget – reflects his absolute commitment to achieving a more secure homeland. The FY 2003 Budget directs $37.7 billion to homeland security, up from $19.5 billion in 2002. This massive infusion of Federal resources reflects the priority the President has attached to the homeland security agenda.

The homeland security portion of the President's 2003 Budget was developed though close cooperation among the Office of Homeland Security, the Office of Management and Budget, and the affected Federal agencies. The Administration intends to provide whatever resources are necessary to secure the homeland, but is committed to ensuring that the taxpayers' money is well spent. Therefore, this year's Budget does not attempt to address the totality of the homeland security agenda, a task that will be more fully developed with the publication of the National Strategy for Homeland Security and the Budget for 2004.

This year's Budget focuses on four specific policy initiatives that were deemed so important and so urgent that they required immediate attention. These initiatives are:

> Supporting First Responders
> Defending Against Bioterrorism
> Securing America's Borders
> Using 21st Century Technology to Secure the Homeland

These initiatives are described in the pages that follow.

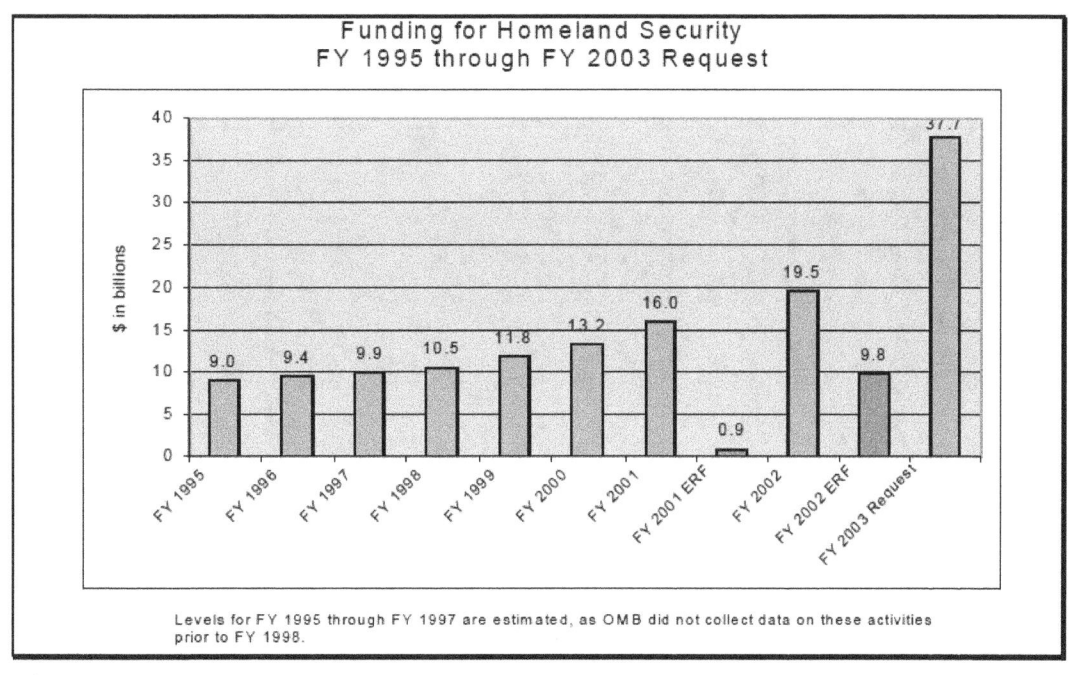

Levels for FY 1995 through FY 1997 are estimated, as OMB did not collect data on these activities prior to FY 1998.

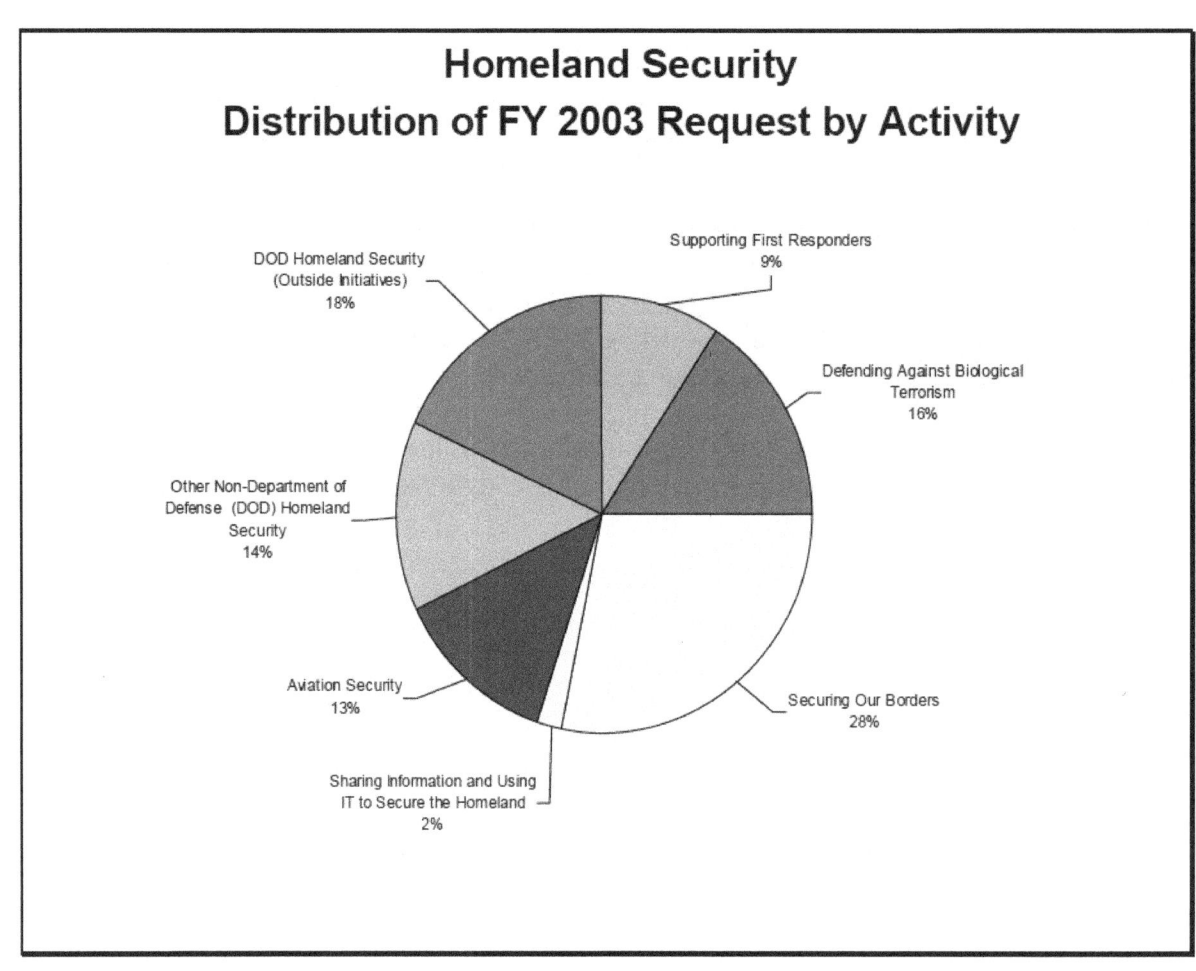

Homeland Security
Distribution of FY 2003 Request by Activity

DOD Homeland Security
(Outside Initiatives)
18%

Supporting First Responders
9%

Defending Against Biological
Terrorism
16%

Other Non-Department of
Defense (DOD) Homeland
Security
14%

Securing Our Borders
28%

Aviation Security
13%

Sharing Information and Using
IT to Secure the Homeland
2%

Supporting First Responders

America's first line of defense in any terrorist attack is the "first responder" community – local police, firefighters, and emergency medical professionals. Properly trained and equipped first responders have the greatest potential to save lives and limit casualties after a terrorist attack. Currently, our capabilities for responding to a terrorist attack vary widely across the country. Many areas have little or no capability to respond to terrorist attack using weapons of mass destruction. Even the best prepared States and localities do not possess adequate resources to respond to the full range of terrorist threats we face.

Facts about First Responders

- There are over 1 million firefighters in the United States, of which approximately 750,000 are volunteers.
- Local police departments have an estimated 556,000 full-time employees including about 436,000 sworn personnel.
- Sheriffs' offices reported about 291,000 full-time employees, including about 186,000 sworn personnel.
- There are over 155,000 nationally registered Emergency Medical Technicians (EMT).

The President's 2003 Budget proposes to spend $3.5 billion on enhancing the homeland security response capabilities of America's first responders – a greater than 10-fold increase in Federal resources. This initiative will accomplish the following objectives:

- Provide the first responder community with much-needed funds to conduct important planning and exercises, purchase equipment, and train their personnel.

- Provide States and localities with the flexibility they require to ensure that the funds are used to address the needs of their local communities.

- Establish a consolidated, simple, and quick method for dispersing Federal assistance to States and localities.

- Encourage mutual aid across the Nation so that the entire local, State, Federal, and volunteer network can operate together effectively.

- Establish a process for evaluating the effort to build response capabilities, in order to validate that effort and direct future resources.

- Encourage citizens to participate actively in preparing their communities for the threat of terrorism and other disastrous events.

To achieve these objectives, the Federal Emergency Management Agency (FEMA) will implement a streamlined and simple procedure designed to speed the flow of resources to the States and localities. The funds may be used for the following types of first responder activities:

- *Planning*. The program will support State and local governments in developing comprehensive plans to prepare for and respond to a terrorist attack.

- *Equipment*. The program will allow State and local first responder agencies to purchase a wide range of equipment needed to respond effectively to a terrorist attack, including personal protective equipment, chemical and biological detection systems, and interoperable communications gear.

- *Training*. The First Responder Initiative will also provide resources to train firefighters, police officers, and emergency medical technicians to respond and operate in a chemical or biological environment.

- *Exercises*. The program will support a coordinated, regular exercise program to improve response capabilities, practice mutual aid, and assess operational improvements and deficiencies.

Strengthening America's first responder community will make our homeland safer. Nearly two million first responders regularly put their lives at risk to save lives and make our country safer. Hundreds of firefighters, police officers and emergency medical workers gave their lives on September 11 as they worked to save others. The First Responder Initiative will help these brave Americans do their jobs better. Building on existing capabilities at the Federal, State, and local level, the First Responder Initiative provides an incentive to develop mutually supportive programs that maximize effective response capability. Through joint planning, clear communication, comprehensive coordination, mutual aid at all levels and increased information sharing, America's first responders can be trained and equipped to save lives in the event of a terrorist attack.

The benefits of building first responder capability are immediate and widespread – making the nation safer from terrorist attacks while also bolstering everyday response capabilities.

Defending Against Biological Terrorism

> Disease has long been the deadliest enemy of mankind. Infectious diseases make no distinctions among people and recognize no borders. We have fought the causes and consequences of disease throughout history and must continue to do so with every available means. All civilized nations reject as intolerable the use of disease and biological weapons as instruments of war and terror.
>
> President George W. Bush
> November 1, 2001

One of the most important missions we have as a Nation is to be prepared for the threat of biological terrorism – the deliberate use of disease as a weapon. An effective biodefense will require a long-term strategy and significant new investment in the U.S. health care system. The President is taking steps now that will significantly improve the Nation's ability to protect its citizens against the threat of bioterrorism. The President's Budget for 2003 proposes $5.9 billion to defending against biological terrorism, an increase of $4.5 billion – or 319 percent – from the 2002 level. This new funding will focus on:

1. **Infrastructure**. Strengthen the State and local health systems, including by enhancing medical communications and disease surveillance capabilities, to maximize their contribution to the overall biodefense of the Nation.

2. **Response**. Improve specialized Federal capabilities to respond in coordination with State and local governments, and private capabilities in the event of a bioterrorist incident and build up the National Pharmaceutical Stockpile.

3. **Science**. Meet the medical needs of our bioterrorism response plans by developing specific new vaccines, medicines, and diagnostic tests through an aggressive research and development program.

Responsibility for detecting and managing a bioterrorist attack needs to be shared among a wide range of Federal, State, local, and private entities. The resources made available in the President's Budget for 2003 will help the Nation develop an effective "early warning" system against a possible bioterrorist attack, and mount an effective operational response to manage its medical consequences. These enhanced capabilities, once in place, will also enhance the Nation's ability to respond to outbreaks of naturally occurring diseases.

Infrastructure: Strengthening America's Public Health System

The President is committed to improving the ability of State and local public health care systems to deal with bioterrorism. State and local public health personnel are a principal line of defense against bioterrorism, and will often be the first to recognize that we are under a biological attack. Ensuring that State and local health care providers have the appropriate tools and the training is critical as our health care community works to carry out this mission.

Many of our health care systems are not adequately prepared for a large-scale attack:

- The health care system lacks the surge capabilities needed to handle quickly large numbers of victims and have insufficient isolation facilities for contagious patients.

- The information system that knits together hospital emergency rooms and public health officials is antiquated and inadequate.

- Little has been done to promote regional mutual aid compacts among health care institutions for bioterrorism attacks.

- Training for health care providers in the handling of bioterrorism victims has been infrequent.

In his 2003 Budget, the President has proposed $1.6 billion to assist State and local health care systems in improving their ability to manage both contagious and non-contagious biological attacks, to expand health care surge capabilities, to upgrade public health laboratory capabilities, and to provide training for medical personnel. The Budget also makes available funding to support the development of regional medical mutual aid compacts. In the event of an emergency, these compacts will enable State and local emergency managers to augment local medical care providers quickly and efficiently. Finally, the communications network that links the acute care providers of our communities with their public health counterparts will be modernized and improved so that vital information on the detection and treatment of disease can flow swiftly.

Response: Enhancing Specialized Federal Capabilities

A major act of biological terrorism would almost certainly overwhelm existing State, local, and privately owned health care capabilities. For this reason, the Federal government maintains a number of specialized response capabilities for a bioterrorist attack. The President's Budget invests $1.8 billion to ensure that these specialized Federal resources are adequate for the threat we face.

The President and the Congress have already taken steps to acquire a national supply of smallpox vaccine and ensure that by the end of fiscal year 2002, the National Pharmaceutical Stockpile will contain sufficient antibiotics to treat 20 million people against diseases such as anthrax, plague and tularemia. The President's Budget for 2003 provides $650 million to carry the process of enhancing the National Pharmaceutical Stockpile even further through:

- The acquisition of the next-generation anthrax vaccine, and the maintenance of and improvements to the national supply of smallpox vaccine. The budget will also provide resources to acquire sufficient amounts of vaccinia immuno globulin (VIG) to treat those that might experience adverse reactions to inoculations.

- Continued maintenance of and improvements to the "push packs" that can be used in the case of both biological and conventional attacks. These pre-assembled packages contain life-saving antidotes, pharmaceuticals, and other medical supplies, and are deployed to the disaster site within 12 hours of a request. The first emergency use of the "push packs" came on September 11 in New York City. In fiscal year 2002, the national supply of these "push packs" was increased from 8 to 12.

- An enhanced vendor managed inventory program so that the Federal government can quickly obtain the additional antibiotics, antidotes, and medical equipment and supplies if an incident requires a larger or multi-phased response.

- Funding support for the States and localities to plan for the receipt and distribution of medicines from the National Pharmaceutical Stockpile.

- The streamlining and integration the Federal bioterrorism response efforts into a unified plan.

Recognizing the potentially global nature of bioterrorism, the Budget for 2003 devotes $10 million to create a team of epidemiological scientists who are committed to working with their counterparts in foreign countries to provide information, research, awareness, and early warning of potential health threats from abroad. Finally, the President's Budget for 2003 provides $20 million to strengthen the Epidemiological Intelligence Service (EIS) at the Centers for Disease Control in Atlanta. Established in 1951 following the start of the Korean War as an early-warning system against biological warfare, the EIS today has expanded into a surveillance and response unit for all types of epidemics.

Science: A New Medical Toolkit for Fighting Bioterrorism

Whether we succeed or fail in our response to an act of bioterrorism depends in large measure on the quality and effectiveness of our diagnostic tests, vaccines, and therapeutic drugs. Our experience responding to the anthrax letter attacks of October 2001 has revealed major inadequacies in our existing medical "toolkit" for fighting bioterrorism. Some of the diagnostics, vaccines, and therapeutics available to us today were developed during the Cold War and hence do not harness the full power of modern biomedical science.

The President's Budget for 2003 devotes $2.4 billion to jump-starting the research and development process needed to provide America with the medical tools needed to support an effective response to bioterrorism. These resources will be focused in the following areas:

- $1.75 billion will be provided to the National Institutes of Health to conduct basic and applied research needed to provide solutions to a range of specific operational problems in our bioterrorism response plans. To do this, NIH will lead a partnership with industry, academia, and government agencies dedicated to understanding the pathogenesis of potential bioterrorism agents and to translating this knowledge into required medical products.

- Over $600 million will be allocated to the Department of Defense, of which $420 million will be used to accelerate efforts to develop better detection, identification, collection, and monitoring technology. Additionally, the scientists working under Defense auspices will support the law enforcement, national security, and medical communities by improving our understanding of how potential bioterrorism pathogens may be weaponized, transported, and disseminated.

- $75 million will go to the Environmental Protection Agency to develop better methods for decontaminating buildings where bioterrorism agents have been released.

Securing America's Borders

America's borders – land, air or sea – are the boundaries between the United States and the rest of the world. The massive flow of people and goods across our borders helps drive our economy, but can also serve as a conduit for terrorists, weapons of mass destruction, illegal migrants, contraband, and other unlawful commodities. The new threats and opportunities of the 21st century demand a new approach to border management. President Bush envisions a border that is grounded on two key principles:

- First, America's air, land, and sea borders must provide a strong defense for the American people against all external threats, most importantly international terrorists but also drugs, foreign disease, and other dangerous items.

- Second, America's border must be highly efficient, posing little or no obstacle to legitimate trade and travel.

The President's 2003 Budget begins the process of achieving this vision of the border of the future.

Facts about America's Borders

- The United States has a 7500-mile land and air border shared with Canada and Mexico and an exclusive economic zone encompassing 3.4 million square miles.
- Each year, more than 500 million people are admitted into the United States, of which 330 million are non-citizens.
- On land, 11.2 million trucks and 2.2 million rail cars cross into the United States, while 7,500 foreign-flag ships make 51,000 calls in U.S. ports annually.

The Smart Border of the Future

America requires a border management system that keeps pace with expanding trade while protecting the United States and its territories from the threats of terrorist attack, illegal immigration, illegal drugs, and other contraband. The border of the future must integrate actions abroad to screen goods and people prior to their arrival in sovereign U.S. territory, and inspections at the border and measures within the United States to ensure compliance with entry and import permits. Federal border control agencies must have seamless information-sharing systems that allow for coordinated communication among themselves, and also the broader law enforcement and intelligence gathering communities. This integrated system would provide timely enforcement of laws and regulations. Agreements with our neighbors, major trading partners, and private industry will allow extensive pre-screening of low-risk traffic, thereby allowing limited assets to focus attention on high-risk traffic. The use of advanced technology to track the movement of cargo and the entry and exit of individuals is essential to the task of managing the movement of hundreds of millions of individuals, conveyances, and vehicles.

Some of this work has already begun with Canada, our largest trading partner. On December 12, 2001, Governor Tom Ridge, Director of the Office of Homeland Security, and John Manley, then Canada's Minister of Foreign Affairs, signed the "Smart Border Declaration" with a 30-point action plan that will help speed and secure the flow of people and goods between the United States and Canada. The Smart Border Declaration recognizes that "our current and future prosperity and security depend on a border that operates efficiently and effectively under all circumstances." A similar effort is currently underway with Mexico.

Border Security Initiatives in the 2003 Budget

In the 2003 Budget, the President will propose approximately $11 billion for border security, including $380 million for the Immigration and Naturalization Service to construct a state of the art Entry-Exit visa system. In total, this will represent an increase of $2.2 billion from the 2002 Budget for border security. This additional funding will allow our border agencies to begin implementing a seamless air, land, and sea border that protects the United States against foreign threats while moving legitimate goods and people into and out of the country. The new border initiatives will be managed by the agencies with primary responsibility for border control.

U.S. Customs Service -- Inspections
The President's 2003 Budget increases the inspection budget of the Customs Services by $619 million, for a total of $2.3 billion. This additional funding increases the ability of the Customs Service to fulfill its critical border security role. Specifically, the additional resources in the 2003 Budget will allow the Customs Service to achieve the following key objectives:

- **Additional Personnel**. The Customs Service will complete the hiring of approximately 800 new inspectors and agents to carry out additional security activities on our borders and at our seaports.

- **New Technology**. The President's Budget provides resources to purchase technologically advanced equipment that will assist in inspecting shipments so that time-consuming and labor-intensive searches can be minimized.

Immigration and Naturalization Service (INS) – Enforcement
The President's 2003 Budget increases the INS budget for enforcement by $1.2 billion, for a total of $5.3 billion, including the resources necessary to implement the Entry-Exit visa system. These resources will enhance key INS missions related to homeland security, including border patrol, inspections, and the implementation of a technologically advanced system for monitoring the entry and exit of foreign visitors. Key goals include:

- **Additional Personnel**. The INS will more than double the number of border patrol agents and inspectors on the northern border. INS will also install integrated information systems to ensure that timely, accurate and complete enforcement data is transmitted to INS agents and other border security agencies operating in the field.

- **Entry–Exit Tracking System**. The INS will implement a new entry-exit system to track the arrival and departure of non-U.S. citizens. This new system will dramatically improve our ability to deny access to those individuals who should not enter the United States, while speeding the entry of routine, legitimate traffic.

United States Coast Guard

The President's 2003 Budget increases funding for the Coast Guard's homeland security-related missions (protecting ports and coastal areas, as well as interdiction activities) by $282 million, to an overall level of $2.9 billion. After September 11, the Coast Guard's port security mission grew from approximately 1-2 percent of daily operations to between 50-60 percent today. In addition, the Coast Guard has important national security missions such as illegal immigration and drug interdiction and port security.

- **Coordination.** Working with other port entities, the Coast Guard is developing tracking mechanisms for all vessels operating in the maritime domain: within or transiting to U.S. ports and transiting our coastal waters. The heart of this maritime domain awareness program is accurate information, intelligence, surveillance, and reconnaissance of all vessels, cargo, and people extending well beyond our traditional maritime boundaries.

- **Coastal Asset and Infrastructure Protection.** Coast Guard forces will provide enhanced defenses for critical high-risk vessels and coastal facilities, marine and otherwise (e.g. nuclear power plants, oil refineries). Close coordination through Harbor Safety Committees, which help bring together the many local, state, and Federal agencies that maintain and protect the harbor, will ensure a well-balanced protective envelope is sustained at different threat levels.

USING 21ST CENTURY TECHNOLOGY TO DEFEND THE HOMELAND

America's information infrastructure is a source of both great strength and considerable vulnerability. The President recognizes that modern information technology is essential not only for making our Nation more prosperous but for making our homeland more secure. The President has launched a long-term program for using advanced information management technology to better protect the Nation. At the same time, the President's 2003 Budget requests significant funding for cyberspace security, an essential new mission for the 21st century given our growing dependence on critical information infrastructure, most importantly the Internet.

Information Technology and the Federal Government: Expanding E-Government

The Budget for 2003 requests a total of $50 billion for information technology investment across the entire Federal government. This enormous Federal investment in technology represents an opportunity to improve the performance of billions of dollars of Federal spending by increasing the effectiveness and efficiency of government.

Led by the Office of Management and Budget, the Administration is deploying 21 high payoff e-government initiatives to maximize Federal government productivity gains from technology, eliminate redundant systems, and significantly improve government's quality of service for citizens, businesses, and other levels of government over the next 18 to 24 months.

Using Information to Secure the Homeland

The President believes that an effective use of intelligence and closer coordination across all levels of government will help stop future terrorist attacks. In the wake of September 11, for example, we discovered that information on the hijackers' activities was available through a variety of databases at the Federal, State, and local government levels as well as within the private sector. Looking forward, we must build a system that combines threat information and then transmits it as needed to all relevant law enforcement and public safety officials.

The President's budget calls for an increase of $722 million and sets in motion a program to use information technology to more effectively share information and intelligence, both horizontally (among Federal agencies and Departments) and vertically (among the Federal, State and local governments). This ongoing homeland security initiative is a key component of the President's "Expanded Electronic Government" management initiative for the entire Federal government, which seeks to improve the way that agencies work together to serve citizens by maximizing the benefits of the Federal government's overall investment in information technology.

The homeland security information initiative has two key objectives:

- **Goal 1: Tear down unwarranted information "stovepipes" within the Federal government.** The President's Budget for 2003 proposes to establish an Information Integration Office within the Department of Commerce to implement a number of priority homeland security goals in the area of horizontal information sharing. The most important function of this office will be to design and help implement an interagency information architecture that will support United States efforts to find, track, and respond to terrorist threats within the United States and around the world, in a way that improves both the time of response and the quality of decisions. Controls will be developed to ensure that this initiative is carried out in a manner consistent with our broader values of civil liberties, economic prosperity, and privacy.

Information technology is also a key to keeping track of short-term foreign visitors. Currently, the country has no system in place for monitoring when a foreign visitor has overstayed his or her visa. To begin filling this gap, the President's 2003 Budget provides $380 million to the INS to implement a new entry-exit system to track the arrival and departure of non-U.S. citizens. This new information-based system will dramatically improve our ability to deny access to those individuals who should not enter the United States, while speeding the entry of routine, legitimate traffic.

- **Goal 2: Share homeland security information with States, localities, and relevant private sector entities.** The struggle against terrorism is a truly national struggle. Federal, State, and local government agencies, as well as the private sector, must work seamlessly together. Having the right system of communication – content, process, and infrastructure – is critical to bridging the existing gaps between the Federal, State, and local governments, as well as the private sector. These new systems will greatly assist our officials at all levels to protect and defend against future terrorist attacks, and to effectively manage incidents whenever they should occur.

To help meet these needs, the Administration will establish a uniform national threat advisory system to inform Federal agencies, State and local officials, as well as the private sector, of terrorist threats and appropriate protective actions. The Budget for 2003 supports this effort by funding the development and implementation of secure information systems to streamline the dissemination of critical homeland security information.

Cyberspace-Security: Protecting our Information Infrastructure

> **The information technology revolution has changed the way business is transacted, government operates and national defense is conducted.** These three functions are now fueled by an interdependent network of critical information infrastructures of which the Internet is key. America must do more to strengthen security on the Internet to protect our critical infrastructure. This cannot be done through government regulation; it can only be accomplished through a voluntary public and private partnership, including corporate and non-governmental organizations.

The President recognized the importance of ensuring the continued operation of America's critical information services by creating a national board and designating a special advisor for cyberspace security. Since October 2001, the President's Critical Infrastructure Protection Board has organized national committees to streamline initiatives and address emergency planning. The board has initiated research into potential methods to isolate and protect critical government information that carries vital communications. It has fostered an unprecedented national government-industry partnership to provide alert and warning for cyberspace threats.

This comprehensive strategy to defend cyberspace will be the result of a true partnership among government and the owners and operatives of critical infrastructure – including our partnership with the information technology industry, telecommunications, electric power, and the financial services industries. Some of the components of this national strategy will include:

National Infrastructure Protection Center (NIPC). The President's Budget for 2003 requests $125 million to fund the NIPC, the premier cyberspace-threat response center located within the FBI. This request represents an increase of more than $50 million from the NIPC's base 2002 funding level.

Cyberspace Warning Intelligence Network. The Internet and our critical infrastructure are constantly under attack from viruses and other invasive programs. The President's Budget for 2003 requests $30 million to create the Cyberspace Warning Intelligence Network (CWIN) that would link the major players in government and the private sector to manage future cyberspace crises.

Priority Wireless Access. On September 11, we learned first hand that in times of a major crisis, wireless communication jams due to congestion. First responders must be able to complete calls in a timely manner. The President's Budget for 2003 requests $60 million to develop a wireless priority access program that will give authorized users priority on the cellular network. The program will ensure that first responders have priority for cellular phone coverage during emergencies.

National Infrastructure Simulation and Analysis Center. The President's Budget for 2003 requests $20 million to fund the National Infrastructure Simulation and Analysis Center at the Department of Energy. This Center will promote collaboration between Federal research efforts and the private sector to better understand the dependencies between the Internet, our critical infrastructure, and our economy.

Secure "GovNet" Feasibility Study. The President's Budget for 2003 requests $5 million for a feasibility study of a proposal to develop a government network that will secure critical functions performed by government at a higher level of security against external attack.

Advanced Encryption Standard. The President helped foster better computer security at Federal agencies. A new Federal standard announced on December 4, 2001, is designed to protect sensitive, unclassified information well into the 21st century. In limited circumstances, it will also be available for classified national security information. The new standard, called the Advanced Encryption Standard, also is expected to be used widely in the private sector, benefiting millions of consumers and businesses.

Cybercorps Scholarships for Serivce. The President's Budget for 2003 requests $11 million for the "Cybercorps." By injecting scholarship funding into universities across America, the Cybercorps Scholarship for Service program encourages college students to become high tech computer security professionals within government. Managed by the National Science Foundation and the Office of Personnel Management, this program also helps to build academic programs at universities in the area of computer security.

Homeland Security: Additional Budget Priorities

The four initiatives in the President's Budget for 2003 are not the totality of the homeland security agenda. Over the course of 2002, the Administration will develop a comprehensive Federal budget plan for securing the homeland, which will systematically address the entire agenda. Yet even before the completion of this plan, virtually every Federal agency has some activity defined as homeland security. Several key activities not mentioned elsewhere include:

Transportation Security

On November 19, 2001, the President signed into law the Aviation and Transportation Security Act, which among other things established a new Transportation Security Administration (TSA) within the Department of Transportation. This Act established a series of challenging but critically important milestones toward achieving a secure air travel system. The President's Budget for 2003 requests $4.8 billion to fulfill the mandates established by the Act.

More broadly however, the Aviation and Transportation Security Act fundamentally changed the way transportation security will be performed and managed in the United States. The continued growth of commercial transportation, tourism and the world economy depends upon effective transportation security measures being efficiently applied. However, the threat to transportation is not restricted solely to those motivated by political or social concerns. In addition to terrorism, TSA will also work to prevent other criminal acts, regardless of motivation.

The Aviation and Transportation Security Act recognized the importance of security for all forms of transportation and related infrastructure elements. This cannot be accomplished by the TSA in isolation and requires strengthened partnerships among Federal, State and local government officials, and the private sector to reduce vulnerabilities and adopt the best practices in use today.

Infrastructure protection of critical assets such as pipelines and more than 10,000 FAA facilities is another key mission of the TSA. Along with rail and highway bridges, many other national assets are critical to our economic and national security and vital for the free and seamless movement of passengers and goods throughout the country.

Federal Law Enforcement

The President's Budget for 2003 will allow the FBI to add more than 300 special agents and other investigative staff to conduct surveillance of terrorists and collect intelligence information about terrorist activities. It will add more than 130 Federal Bureau of Investigation special agents and other investigative staff specifically to combat cyber-crime and protect our banking, finance, energy, transportation, and other critical systems from disruption by terrorists. It will also provide Drug Enforcement Agency with more than 25 financial crime investigators to help identify and shut down the sources of money that support the terrorist cells.

Citizen Corps

The Citizen Corps will enable Americans to volunteer to participate directly in homeland security efforts in their own communities. Citizen Corps will be coordinated by the Federal Emergency Management Agency (FEMA).

The President's Budget for fiscal year 2003 requests $144 million in matching funds to support the formation and training of local Citizen Corps Councils. These community-based Citizen Corps Councils will help drive local involvement in Citizen Corps, developing community action plans, assessing possible threats, identifying local resources and coordinating other Citizen Corps programs. These Councils will be broad-based – including leaders from law enforcement, fire and emergency medical services, businesses, community-based institutions, schools, places of worship, health care facilities, public works and other key community sectors.

Citizen Corps volunteers will be able to participate in a variety of programs that match their skills and abilities. The President's fiscal year 2003 Budget provides more than $230 million for these efforts, including:

➢ *Volunteers in Police Service (VIPS) Program:* Builds on successful local programs in which civilian volunteers help local police departments to perform non-sworn functions, freeing up police officers to perform vital front-line duties in times of emergency.

➢ *Medical Reserve Corps:* Enables retired healthcare professionals to effectively augment local health officials' capacity to respond to an emergency.

➢ *Operation TIPS (Terrorist Information and Prevention System):* Operation TIPS will enable millions of America transportation workers, postal workers, and public utility employees to identify and report suspicious activities linked to terrorism and crime.

➢ *Community Emergency Response Teams (CERT):* The President has proposed tripling over the next two years the number of Americans enrolled in CERT – a training program that enables individual Americans to participate in emergency management planning in their communities and prepare to respond to disasters and other emergencies.

➢ *Neighborhood Watch Programs:* The President's plan will double the number of Neighborhood Watch Programs in the next two years, and enhance the program by incorporating terrorism prevention into its mission.

➢ *Citizens' Preparedness Guidebook:* The Citizens' Preparedness Guidebook provides current crime and disaster preparedness techniques as well as the latest information on terrorism, to give Americans guidance on how to prepare in their homes, neighborhoods, workplaces and public spaces.

Department of Defense and Intelligence Community

The President's Budget for 2003 requests $7.8 billion for homeland security-related activities of the Department of Defense and Intelligence Community. The largest portion of the total request ($4.6 billion) is dedicated to the physical security of Department of Defense facilities and personnel inside the United States, while the second largest is for maintaining combat air patrols within U.S. airspace ($1.3 billion). The Budget for 2003 also requests significant funding for research and development related to combating terrorism, as well as for several specialized response teams such as the National Guard's Weapons of Mass Destruction Civil Support Teams.

Protecting our Critical Infrastructure

After September 11, the Administration took a wide range of urgent steps to protect the Nation's highest risk targets and critical infrastructure systems – such as nuclear power plans, ports, hydroelectric dams, telecommunications nodes, border crossings, and chemical facilities. This effort proceeded in cooperation with many different State and local agencies and private companies. Over the longer term, however, the Administration recognizes the need to address the security of America's highest risk targets and critical infrastructure systems in a comprehensive fashion. Accordingly, the Administration has begun a systematic effort to define, prioritize, and develop effective strategies for protecting the Nation's critical infrastructure. This framework will produce the country's first unified critical infrastructure protection plan, with full involvement by all relevant Federal agencies as well as State and local governments and private industry.

Additional Data and Charts

How the Homeland Security Budget was Calculated

Homeland Security encompasses those activities that are focused on combating terrorism and occur within the United States and its territories. Such activities include efforts to detect, deter, protect against and, if needed, respond to terrorist attacks.

As a starting point, funding estimates for these activities are based on data that has been reported since 1998 in the Office of Management and Budget's *Annual Report to Congress on Combating Terrorism,* and include combating terrorism and weapons of mass destruction (WMD), critical infrastructure protection (CIP), and continuity of operations (COOP).

Since homeland security focuses on activities within the United States, estimates do not include costs associated with fighting terrorism overseas; those costs are captured within the war on terrorism abroad category. In addition, homeland security estimates include all funding associated with border security (i.e., Immigration and Naturalization Service's enforcement and detention activities, the Customs Service enforcement activities, the Coast Guard's enforcement activities, the Agricultural Quarantine Inspection Program, and the Department of State's visa program) and aviation security.

The Office of Management and Budget's Combating Terrorism report defines combating terrorism and WMD preparedness, CIP, and COOP. Combating terrorism includes both antiterrorism, defensive measures used to combat terrorism, and counterterrorism, offensive measures used to combat terrorism, and includes the following five categories of activities:

- law enforcement and investigative activities;
- preparing for and responding to terrorist acts;
- physical security of government facilities and employees;
- physical protection of national populace and national
- infrastructure; and,
- research and development.

CIP is defined as efforts associated with enhancing the physical and cybersecurity of public and private sector infrastructures, especially cyber systems that are so vital to the Nation that their incapacitation or destruction would have a debilitating impact on national security, national economic security, and/or national public health and safety.

COOP refers to the capability of Federal agencies to perform essential functions during any emergency or situation that may disrupt normal operations.

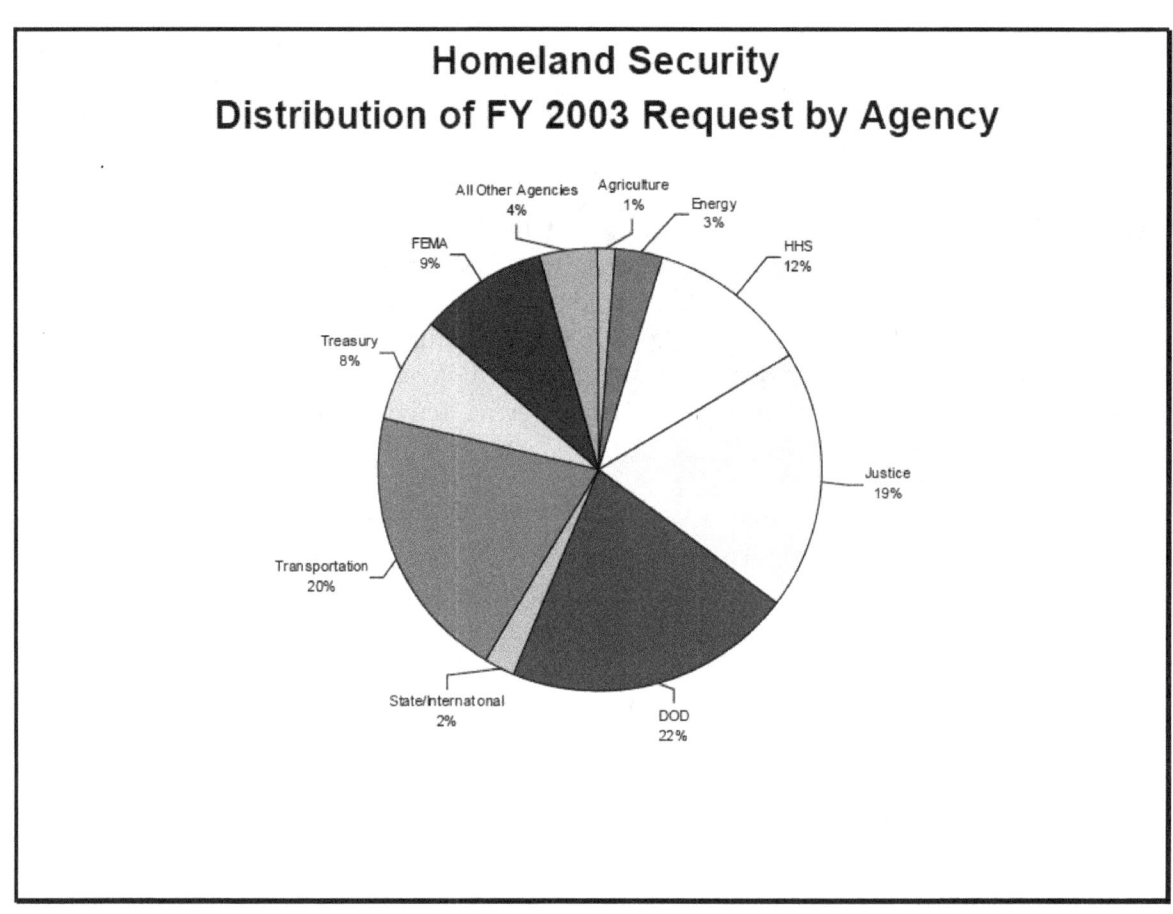

**Homeland Security
Distribution of FY 2003 Request by Agency**

All Other Agencies 4%

Agriculture 1%

Energy 3%

HHS 12%

FEMA 9%

Treasury 8%

Justice 19%

Transportation 20%

State/International 2%

DOD 22%

Homeland Security -- Funding by Initiative Area
($ in millions)

	2002 Enacted Base	FY 2002 Supp.	FY 2003 Proposed
Supporting First Responders	291	651	3,500
Defending Against Biological Terrorism	1,408	3,730	5,898
Securing America's Borders	8,752	1,194	10,615
Using 21st Century Technology to Defend the Homeland	155	75	722
Aviation Security	1,543	1,035	4,800
Other Non-Department of Defense (DOD) Homeland Security	3,186	2,384	5,352
DOD Homeland Security (Outside Initiatives)	4,201	689	6,815
Total	19,535	9,758	37,702

Supporting First Responders

($ in millions)

FEMA/Justice:	2002 Enacted Base *	FY 2002 Supp. *	FY 2003 Proposed
Equip First Responder Teams	159	188	770
Train State and Local First Responders	56	171	665
Assist Emergency Response Planning	3	24	35
Enhance Communications Infrastructure to Support Interoperability	0	113	1,365
Improve Command and Control to Ensure Effective Procedures at Response Sites	0	17	35
Fund Interjurisdictional Agreements and Mutual Aid Compacts	0	0	140
Disseminate Information Regarding Emergency Response to the Public	0	0	35
Provide Federal Technical Assistance to State and Local Emergency Response Agencies	36	30	350
Test Readiness and Provide Feedback on Performance	7	85	105
Other	30	25	0
TOTAL, FIRST RESPONDERS	**291**	**651**	**3,500**

* Funds for FY 2002 represent funding for both FEMA ($39 M base and no funds in the supplemental) and Justice ($252 M base and $651 million in the supplemental). All funds for FY 2003 are requested in FEMA.

Note: proposed allocations by activity reflect approximate percentage allocations with adjustments where funding was for mixed activities or not provided. The proposal for FY 2003 provides state and local governments flexibility to target funds to their

Defending Against Biological Terrorism *
($ in millions)

	2002 Enacted Base	FY 2002 Supp.	FY 2003 Proposed
Enhance Medical Communications and Surveillance Capabilities			
Info/Communications Systems	34	40	202
Medical Surveillance Systems	0	0	175
Epidemiologist Exchange Program	0	0	10
Media/Public Information Campaign	0	0	5
Total	**34**	**40**	**392**
Strengthen State and Local Health Systems **			
Hospital Infrastructure (Labs & Decon)	0	0	283
State Public Health Lab Capacity	13	15	200
Hospital Mutual Aid (Planning/Coordination)	5	135	235
State Epidemiological Teams	0	0	80
Educational Incentives for Curriculum	0	0	60
Hospital Training Exercises with States	0	0	73
Public Health Preparedness Planning	29	810	210
Metropolitan Medical Response System (MMRS)	20	0	60
Total	**67**	**960**	**1,202**
Research & Development			
Basic and Applied Biodefense Research (NIH)	93	85	1,080
Biodefense Research Infrastructure (NIH)	0	70	336
Anthrax Vaccine Development (NIH & CDC)	18	0	268
Expedited Drug Approval/Research (FDA)	7	41	49
Research Facility Security Upgrades (HHS)	0	84	100
Bio weapons defense/countermeasures (DOD)			120
Agent Identification, Detection & Area Monitoring (DOD)			300
Other Research and Development (DOD)	182	1	182
Total	**300**	**281**	**2,435**
Improve Federal Response			
National Pharmaceutical Stockpile	52	593	300
Upgrade CDC Capacity & Labs - Including BL 4 Lab	18	60	109
Ft. Collins (HHS)	0	0	100
Improving Decontamination Methods (EPA)	0	0	75
Federal Public Health Response Teams	6	45	43
Federal Preparedness Planning	0	0	10
Total	**76**	**698**	**637**
Other Bioterrorism Preparedness			
Smallpox Vaccine Purchase	0	512	100
FDA Food Safety	0	97	99
HHS Rapid Toxic Screening	5	10	15
Other HHS	43	40	118
EPA Drinking Water Safety	2	88	22
Postal Service Decontamination	0	675	0
Procurement of Biodefense Equipment and Counterproliferation (DOD)	337	63	337
Other Agencies and Activities	544	266	542
TOTAL, BIOTERRORISM	**1,408**	**3,730**	**5,898**

* Does not include funding in the First Responder initiative.

** Total for state and local assistance in FY 2003 is $1.6 billion, which includes funding for communications/surveillance systems, and to assist state and local receipt and delivery of national pharmaceutical stockpile supplies.

Securing America's Borders

($ in millions)

	2002 Enacted Base	FY 2002 Supp.	FY 2003 Proposed
Immigration and Naturalization Service (Department of Justice): Enforcement *	**4,111**	**570**	**4,963**
Select components:			
Border Patrol	1,256	68	1,471
Inspections	821	125	999
Detention and Deportation	1,029	10	1,100
Unspecified emergency response requirements (supplemental funding only)		72	
Entry-Exit Visa System (non-add)	*17*	*13*	*380*
INS Including Entry Exit Visa System	*4,128*	*583*	*5,343*
United States Customs Service (Treasury): Inspections	**1,713**	**364**	**2,332**
Select components:			
Northern Border Security	532	117	744
Customs Maritime Security	355	109	684
United States Coast Guard (Transportation): Enforcement	**2,631**	**209**	**2,913**
Select components:			
Ports, Waterways, and Coastal Security	473	209	1,213
Interdiction Activities	778	0	587
Capital Programs	636	0	725
Animal and Plant Health Inspection Service (USDA): Agricultural Quarantine Program (border inspections)	**297**	**50**	**407**
TOTAL, BORDER SECURITY	**8,752**	**1,194**	**10,615**
Total, including Entry-Exit Visa System	*8,769*	*1,207*	*10,995*

* For FY 2003, includes $615 million proposed to be transferred to the detention trustee.

Using 21st Century Technology to Defend the Homeland
($ in millions)

	2002 Enacted Base	FY 2002 Supp.	FY 2003 Proposed
Assure broad access and horizontal sharing across selected Federal databases:			
Program Office to identify and commence process for information sharing (Commerce)	0	0	20
Ensure procedures for and handling of sensitive homeland security information to facilitate information sharing while protecting sources:			
Secure videoconferencing with States (FEMA)*	0	0	7
Entry-Exit Visa System (also represented as a non-add to the Border Initiative -- Funding to INS)	17	13	380
Assure relevant information about threats is conveyed to State and local officials in a timely manner:	3	0	17
Threat Dissemination Systems (Justice)	3	0	10
Educational program for State and local officials (National Archives and Records Administration)	0	0	7
Cyberspace Security: Protecting our Information Infrastructure	135	62	298
National Infrastructure Simulation and Analysis Center (Energy) **	0	0	20
Cyber Warning Intelligence Network (DOD)	0	0	30
Priority Wireless Access (DOD)	0	0	60
GovNet Feasibility Study (GSA)	0	0	5
Cybercorps (NSF)	11	0	11
Federal Computer Incident Response Capability (GSA)	10	0	11
National Infrastructure Protection Center (NIPC) (FBI)	72	61	125
Computer Security Division (NIST)	11	0	15
Critical Infrastructure Assurance Office (Commerce)	5	1	7
Other IT/Information Sharing	26	0	15
TOTAL, IT/INFORMATION SHARING	**155**	**75**	**722**

* Includes funding under the First Responder Initiative.

** Does not include $20 million in supplemental funding provided to DOD for the NISAC. Funds are included in the DOD total.

Homeland Security -- Non-Defense Funding Outside of Initiative Areas
($ in millions)

	2002 En. Base	FY 2002 Supp.	FY 2003 Proposed
Department of Agriculture: Physical and IT Security	12	106	94
Department of Commerce: Physical Security, IT Security, and CIP	73	16	88
Department of Energy: Energy Security, Physical Security, IT Security, and R&D (non-Bioterrorism)	744	142	884
Department of the Interior, Safeguarding Facilities and National Landmarks	26	89	94
International Agencies: Domestic Physical Security and Visa Programs	618	80	814
Department of Justice: Law Enforcement and Other Activities	585	809	1,643
Department of Transportation: Hardening Modes (non-aviation) and Research and Development	7	132	14
Department of the Treasury: Law Enforcement and Other Activities	386	251	521
Corps of Engineers: Hardening and Security	0	139	65
Executive Office of the President: Physical and IT Security and the Office of Homeland Security	2	58	48
FEMA: Salaries and Expenses and the Office of National Preparedness	0	25	50
GSA: Federal Facilities Security	109	127	326
NASA: Security of Assets	121	109	129
NSF: CIP Research and Physical and IT Security	198	0	197
SSA: Critical Infrastructure Protection	102	3	119
Corporation for National and Community Service	29	0	118
DC: Emergency Planning and Response for the Capitol Region	13	200	15
Nuclear Regulatory Commission	5	36	34
Other Homeland Security	157	63	99
TOTAL, OTHER HOMELAND SECURITY	3,186	2,384	5,352